Whose Opinion is Right

and

The Painful Truth

by

A Friend of Medjugorje

feature articles of the July through December, 1993 edition
of the Caritas of Birmingham newsletter

No attempt is intended to pre-empt the Church on the validity of the Apparitions. They are private revelation awaiting the Church's judgment. Because the Queen of Peace Apparitions are ongoing and not yet over, the Church has yet to rule on their authenticity. Caritas of Birmingham, the Community of Caritas and all associated with it, realize and accept that the final authority regarding the Queen of Peace Medjugorje Apparitions rests with the Holy See in Rome. We at Caritas, willingly submit to that judgment. Caritas of Birmingham and its mission is not connected to the Diocese of Birmingham, Alabama. The Diocese of Birmingham's official position on Caritas is neutral and holds us as Catholics in good standing.

For additional copies write:

Caritas of Birmingham
100 Our Lady Queen of Peace Drive
Sterrett, AL 35147 USA
Call 205-672-2000 press ext. 315 (24 hours a day)
See pages 79–80 for Pricing.

ABOUT THE AUTHOR

The author of this book is also the author of the books <u>Words From Heaven</u>®, <u>How to Change Your Husband</u>™, <u>I See Far</u>™, <u>Look What Happened While You Were Sleeping</u>™, <u>It Ain't Gonna Happen</u>™ and other publications such as the *Words of the Harvesters* and the *Caritas of Birmingham Newsletter*. He has written more on Medjugorje than anyone in the world, producing life-changing writings and spiritual direction to countless numbers across the world, of all nationalities. He wishes to be known only as "A Friend of Medjugorje." The author is not one looking in from the outside regarding Medjugorje, but one who is close to the events - many times, right in the middle of the events about which he has written; a first-hand witness.

Originally writing to only a few individuals in 1987, readership has grown to over 250,000 in the United States, with additional readers in over one hundred thirty foreign countries, who follow the spiritual insights and direction given through these writings.

The author, when asked why he signs only as "A Friend of Medjugorje," stated:

> *"I have never had an ambition or desire to write. I do so only because God has shown me, through prayer, that He desires this of me. So from the beginning, when I was writing to only a few people, I prayed to God and promised I would not sign anything; that the writings would have to carry themselves and not be built on a personality. I prayed*

*that if it was God's desire for these writings to be
inspired and known, then He could do it by His
Will and grace and that my will be abandoned to it.*

*"The Father has made these writings known and
continues to spread them to the ends of the earth.
These were Our Lord's last words before ascend-
ing:* ***"Be a witness to the ends of the earth."***
*These writings give testimony to that desire of Our
Lord to be a witness with one's life. It is not important to be known. It is important to do God's Will."*

For those who require "ownership" of these writings by the
author in seeing his name printed on this work in order to give
it more credibility, we state that we cannot reconcile the fact
that these writings are producing hundreds of thousands of
conversions, if not millions through grace, and are requested
worldwide from every corner of the earth. The author, therefore, will not take credit for a work that, by proof of the impact
these writings have to lead hearts to conversion, have been
Spirit–inspired with numbers increasing yearly, sweeping as a
wave across the ocean. Indeed in this case, crossing every
ocean of the earth. Our Lady gave this author a direct message
for him through the visionary, Marija, of Medjugorje, in which
Our Lady said to him to witness not with words but through
humility. It is for this reason that he wishes to remain simply
"A Friend of Medjugorje."

— Caritas of Birmingham

Medjugorje

The Story in Brief

THE VILLAGE SEES THE LIGHT is the title of a story which "Reader's Digest" published in February 1986. It was the first major news on a mass public scale that told of the Virgin Mary visiting the tiny village of Medjugorje, Bosnia-Hercegovina. At that time this village was populated by 400 families.

It was June 24, 1981, the Feast of John the Baptist, the proclaimer of the coming Messiah. In the evening, around 5:00 p.m., the Virgin Mary appeared to two young people, Mirjana Dragičević* and Ivanka Ivanković*. Around 6:40 p.m. the same day, Mirjana and Ivanka, along with four more young people, Milka Pavlović*, the little sister of Marija, Ivan Ivanković, Vicka Ivanković*, and Ivan Dragičević saw the Virgin Mary. The next day, June 25, 1981, along with Mirjana, Ivanka, Vicka and Ivan Dragičević, Marija Pavlović* and Jakov Čolo also saw the Virgin Mary, bringing the total to six visionaries. Milka Pavlović* and Ivan Ivanković only saw Our Lady once, on that first day. These six have become known as and remain "the visionaries."

These visionaries are not related to one another. Three of the six visionaries no longer see Our Lady on a daily basis. As of April 2011, the Virgin is still appearing everyday to the remaining three visionaries; that's well over 13,479 apparitions.

* Names at the time of the apparitions, they are now married with last names changed.

The supernatural event has survived all efforts of the Communists to put a stop to it, many scientific studies, and even the condemnation by the local bishop; yet, the apparitions have survived, giving strong evidence that this is from God because nothing and no one has been able to stop it. For over twenty-nine years, the apparitions have proved themselves over and over and now credibility is so favorable around the world that the burden of proof that this is authentic has shifted from those who believe to the burden of proof that it is not happening by those opposed to it. Those against the apparitions are being crushed by the fruits of Medjugorje — millions and millions of conversions which are so powerful that they are changing and will continue to change the whole face of the earth.

See **mej.com** for more information.

Whose Opinion Is Right?

The following will change your whole outlook on your life. We believe this segment and the next you read are among the most important writings we've produced. Deep prayer to the Holy Spirit is necessary to grasp what it is God wishes to tell you through what you are about to read. Those in community* here, who proofed these articles, said when they prayed to the Holy Spirit before reading that they deeply felt the presence of the Holy Spirit and Our Lady in a powerful way. We believe for you it will be the same and that "today" is the time to announce these truths anew. The following:

Whose opinion is right? How are opinions formed? How do we conclude which opinion to adopt?

Today, people make their decisions based on what they "feel" is right. Everyone wants to do what is right for himself. Everyone has an opinion about what is right and what is wrong. Many ask, *"Who is anyone to tell another how to live or what is right?" "How dare you tell me what values to have?" "Who do you think you are to impose your beliefs on me?" "I am a good person. I am not bad!"* Yet, who is right? Where is the truth? Truth, today, is based on people's opinions, and their opinions are based on feelings. Feelings are influenced in today's society by advertisements, editorials, billboards, music, friends, university professors, and a host of other material, people, and institutions "melting" out millions of variations of

---

* A community of individuals and families whose lives are consecrated and based on living Our Lady's messages and whose work is dedicated to spreading Our Lady's messages, is located at Caritas of Birmingham.

truth. Relative truth is truth that has to do with your circumstances, and it is your truth. It is "related" to you personally and may not be related to the lifestyle or conditions of others. People say you must be informed. Educate yourself about the issues to know how to form your opinions. So today there are many people believing differently yet believing their beliefs are right because they base them on their own "relative" truth. In today's world there is no absolute truth, rather, many truths. Not having absolutes means having many things you can believe. In other words, *"I believe this way, you believe that way."* This is what most believe in society today. People are erratic and led by their feelings. For instance, a person living an abominable life-style contrary to God's natural law sees that he himself has values because he lives by a "code" or "standard" which he views as normal. In other words, one living in degradation might say, *"I would never run a red light or commit murder—those things are wrong!"* Yet, all the while practicing an abomination. One truth of one individual and another truth for the next person is what society is guided by, "thinking" everyone must live by his own truth which is based on what he feels. There is no final truth, rather a flexible truth to believe many things according to what one or others feel. This flexible truth has now become so changeable it has become fluid. "Fluid" truth or "flexible" truth is shown even by our former president, Bill Clinton. In 1986, he wrote the letter on the following page.

State of Arkansas

Office of the Governor
State Capitol
Little Rock 72201

Bill Clinton
Governor

September 26, 1986

Earlene Windsor
Arkansas Right to Life
P.O. Box 1697
Little Rock, AR 72203

Dear Mrs. Windsor:

Thank you for giving me the opportunity to respond
to the Arkansas Right to Life questionnaire. However,
most of the questions address federal issues outside the
authority of a governor or the state.

Because many of the questions do concern the issue of
abortion, I would like for your members to be informed
of my position on the state's responsibility in that area.
I am opposed to abortion and to government funding of
abortions. We should not spend state funds on abortion
because so many people believe abortion is wrong. I do
support the concept of the proposed Arkansas Constitu-
tional amendment 65 and agree with its stated purpose.
As I have said, I am concerned that some questions
about the amendment's impact appear to remain unan-
swered.

Again, Thank you for allowing me to share my position
on this important issue.

Sincerely,

Bill Clinton

Bill Clinton
BC:kt

9

Notice Clinton says many people "believe it wrong" for the state to fund abortions and indicated his position based on truths which he based on others'. (Even though they are right about abortion, this shows Clinton bases his opinions on people's.) When he was president, <u>his</u> truth changed because, again, he based it on people's opinion who based it on feelings. Today's society has to get a Gallop Poll to know in what to believe. People have become so influenced that many form their opinions even from lies because, through time, satan has deceived a multitude into believing that these lies are right. What was clearly wrong for generations is now right because people feel it is.

You may think, *"At least I know I have values. I know what is right. I am a Christian."* We, as Christians, have to accept a great deal of the guilt and cannot have the attitude that we've based everything we do in "absolute" truth because we haven't. We ourselves have strayed and many devoted Christians base too much on their feelings. This is a gross error. We have to base our lives and form our opinions and our beliefs on truths, not feelings. We have Christians going to Church who believe abortion is not for them but may be okay for others. They think they have no right to impose their beliefs on others. Country singer, Garth Brooks, is a perfect example of this seriously incorrect thinking. He reports to love the Bible; *News Week* states that Garth takes a brave stand. Country music mega star says:

> *"If your parents are the same (gender), that's still a traditional family value to me… It is tough for me because I love the Bible. Are those people*

who feel religiously that (illicit alternative life-style) is wrong not as right as people who feel (an alternative lifestyle) is right?"

What is this opinion based on? It's not truth, it's feelings.

Jesus stood before Pilate and said, ***"The reason I was born, the reason why I came into the world is to 'testify' to the truth. Anyone committed to the truth hears my voice."*** Something incredible happened after that. Imagine Pilate standing there in front of Jesus, and he looks Jesus eye to eye and says, *"Truth!! What does that mean?"* This is incredible because it shows the same situation that existed 2,000 years ago exists today. Pilate, in his position, was knowledgeable and knew that there were many truths, so whose truth do you go with? Who is right? Is our situation not unlike that during Jesus' time? Who or what is testifying to the truth? Few today know whose or what truth to believe. Another translation of Pilate's question is, *"What is truth?"* This question, posed by Pilate, is exactly what this article is about. How do we know what the truth is? Not opinions and flexible truth but "the absolute truth." Our Lady tells us:

June 16, 1983

"I have come to tell the world that God is 'truth'…"

So, knowing and believing this message, how will it help me to know how to form my opinions? Because if God is the truth, then His precepts are the truth. If His precepts are the truth, then so is His "Word." His Word is the Holy Bible. It is why Our Lady has repeatedly told us to read it. It is absolute in truth. Then, too, is not the Church which is grounded in Scriptures, and the Scriptures which are a historical record of the early Church "absolute" in truth? Can truth beget a lie? No. Then why is it so many disregard the Church's dogmas and its head yet still want to belong to it? In 1994, the reigning Miss America stated in *USA Today*, *"I'm a Christian who is pro-choice."* On what does she base this? Nothing. It does not exist. For her and Garth Brooks, as well as many others, beliefs exist only in what they feel which is influenced by opinions—their own and others'. They stand on nothing absolute, rather they stand on flexible beliefs. We must realize many, many opinions today are wrong, even if a poll tells us 90% of the people believe such and such. If these beliefs conflict with the Scriptures, they are wrong.

To find out in what to believe and to be right about our opinions we must turn to the Bible and put our family upon it as our foundation of belief and follow it. For those who want to stand on something absolute and learn not what to feel, but on what to base their opinions, in what to believe, how to act, and what is proper behavior, the Bible is the source. It contains every answer to every problem man has. Society wastes immeasureable amounts of time on help magazines, articles, programs, "Dear Abby's," Ann Lander's, Donahue's and similar programs, etc., when the answers can be found in one small book. The beautiful thing is we do not have to worry if it's the right advice.

There are Christian parents who feel they should tread on eggshells in teaching their children beliefs because they will have to make up their own minds anyway. It is true. They will. If you don't ground them in the Scriptures and Church teachings when they are young, don't wonder why they don't choose your faith later. Children do not have the "right" to choose what truth to follow. It is ridiculous for parents to possess the thought, *"I don't want to impose too much on them. They need to make up their own mind."* Yes, it has to ultimately be their decision to continue the invitation to follow Christ, but you lay the ground work for their saying, "Yes."

One famous movie-star admitted recently, *"I made a terrible mistake not raising my children believing in God and taking them to church."* One may think, *"God has converted non-believers before in miraculous ways; so why worry about people straying as non-believers?"* These writings do not discount the power of God to convert heathens. History has shown over and over that this happens. Rather, it is addressed to us who are Christians already, and for Christians and their families to stray is a tragedy.

Today, "reasons" for doing something are led and completely dominated by feelings. It is supposed to be the opposite. Reason has to dominate feelings and guide them. The Bible says in Isaiah, ***"Come let us reason together."*** Another translation says, ***"Come, now let us set things right."*** Today is the time to set things right. Christians have to "think," reason "through their beliefs," compare them to Scriptures and the Church laws and see if they run parallel or conflict. Change those opinions and beliefs which contradict. Once we do, be ready to enjoy peace no matter how bad the situation is around us. People will be attracted to your way, and they will abandon their truths and Our Lady's ranks will swell.

Finding these truths, running around pronouncing them to the whole world, even obeying them and believing that they make us right, will do us no good just because they are absolute. We gain nothing by this except the title, "Pharisee." We must follow them out of love because we love Him from who they originate. And, if out of fear of offending Him, our love incites us to obey them, then we've gained everything.

You might say *"Garth Brooks and Miss America are way out. Why should I accept some of the guilt for not standing on truth? I stand squarely on it!"* Do you? Many of you may say, *"I believe the Bible and the Church. None of this applies to me."* The whole purpose of this article is to help you understand the next article. Truth can be very painful, and the next article was not written to harm anyone, rather we believe it is time Our Lady wants truth to be spoken. Before going to the next article, it is important to pray. Literally, get on your knees and ask God to give you the Spirit of Truth. On June 9, 1984, Our Lady said:

"...pray for the Spirit of Truth!...Pray for the Holy Spirit to inspire you with the spirit of prayer..."

The Bible tells us:

"When the Spirit of Truth comes, He will guide you into all the truth." John 16:13

In the next article, you will see that perhaps we, as Christians, haven't stood up to and followed the truth as we should, and we all suffer because of it through a dysfunctional society. This has happened through a dysfunctional family life. Now Our Lady is here to help us bear the weight and the pain of the truth so that we may have a mother close by to whom we can go, and cry, and say, *"Help me, help me,"* and have our distress relieved. For many, we know tears will be shed because of what the following article says, so please do not dare enter into it without serious prayer. Pause and ask Our Lady to be with you. Go into it with an open heart. Rid yourself of all worthless opinions. Be ready to change your feelings and opinions and accept God's words from the Scriptures, from His Church, and from His saints. We believe so seriously that prayer is needed for what follows that for the next several months our community will pray daily for all those who will be reading these pages, on that particular day that you will be shown a great spiritual depth of truth about yourself, your family and your situation, and what God's Will is for you.

The Painful Truth

The following is written to you, especially those who are working for the rebirth and awakening of the Church, in the same spirit in which letters were sent to the early Christian communities and extols you to radically change your lives. St. Paul says to the Corinthians:

> ***"I want to give you solid food but I have to give you baby's milk because you are men of flesh and not men of the Spirit."*** 1 Cor. 3:1–3

So what follows is solid food for men of the Spirit; for those of the flesh it may be too much for you to digest and could cause you to choke. Therefore, we appeal to all of you to pray so that your spirit will be able to accept truth that is for the spirit. There are things <u>written</u> "and" purposely <u>unwritten</u> so the Holy Spirit can tell you that which words do not. Both will speak to you to a strong degree about your present situation only if you pray to the Holy Spirit before you begin.

* * * * * * * * * * * *

They had been close friends, traveling to many places together and even visiting part of former Yugoslavia known as Macedonia. Both had been converted and become Christians. The first friend was responsible for the conversion of the other. He wrote to his friend about how important it was not to follow "myths" and "wives tales" but only sound doctrine. That letter was Paul's letter to Timothy, written 2000 years ago, warning that there would come a "certain time" when man would stray and no longer follow the truths which God delivered through His Son. **All** indications… **all evidence** is showing that we have entered that time about which Paul told Timothy. He writes:

> *"For the time will come when people will not tolerate sound doctrine, but following their own desires, will surround themselves with teachers who tickle their ears. They will stop listening to the truth and wander off to fables."* 2 Tim. 4:3–4

Paul also said:

> *"All Scripture is inspired of God and is useful for teaching, for reproof, correction, and training in holiness."* 2 Tim. 3:16

These above two truths are to be <u>remembered as you read on.</u>

* * * * * * * * * * * *

James (not his real name) was a Eucharistic Minister going into the confessional for his regular confession. Little did he realize that when he walked out, he would be devastated. What the priest told him left him in shock. James told the priest of his divorce and his efforts to stay with his wife. Yet she left, and divorce followed. James remarried and had a child with his second wife. The priest told him that he was very sorry about his circumstances, but that he was currently living in a state of sin (adultery) and, therefore, was not able to receive absolution. James was stunned. He thought, *"Why had no one taught me that? Why hadn't the priest, who I knew so well, instructed me?"* James had no idea that his situation was wrong until the one priest stated the truth, however painful, and told him. James recounted, *"I went to my Church and was before the Eucharist weeping, crying real tears of repentance and wanting to do what was right, but knowing I had remarried. My situation was all tangled up. Later when I talked to my parish priest and told him I could no longer be a Eucharistic Minister or receive Holy Communion, he responded back that I should not worry, he would give me absolution. He said the other priest was wrong."* James refused his offer because he had looked into the why's and found out the priest who refused to give him absolution was right. Since the confession, over a year ago, James still has not received the Eucharist, knowing to do so while in sin is wrong. Yet his prayers and sacrifices have been answered in that his first wife who had abortions, among other things, has miraculously given him a "no contest" on his annulment papers. He thought this would never happen because by doing so she admitted his reasons for seeking annulment were correct. As of this writing, James is still waiting.

Why is Church Teaching so strong about the indissolubility of marriage? Why has the Vatican recently called for more restrictive measures to lower the numbers regarding granting annulments, especially in the United States? Our Lady is teaching us many things through Her messages and the following will help you see these truths are based on the "absolutes"—the Scriptures. The whole issue of family life and what's "right" is emotionally packed and built on what people feel rather than the truth. Many will even become angry when one tries to give out—not opinions, but real truth about marriage and its "purpose" and "structure." satan has complicated and suppressed the truth so much that many no longer know the truth, as was the situation with James. Thus satan has suppressed many a pulpit into silence because of the risk of offending those who have divorced or who have remarried without annulments. Some situations are tragic and merit our compassion which is necessary but not to the degree that it hinders the truth. One priest in Florida recounted to us that he spoke about this and birth control, and many began to leave his parish. His donations dropped, and he was pressured into silence. The following is to address everyone in every state of life.

Marriage today and its meaning have become clouded. At the wedding feast of Cana, Jesus's first miracle takes place. It is interesting that Jesus took water and made it into wine. This miracle was an incredible statement of what happens in a marriage. Once Jesus joined His Will to the water, wine was made. It was a befitting miracle for a wedding because even if one wanted to, no one could separate the water that is in the wine and return it to its original state. Since this took place at a <u>wedding</u>, this miracle defines the <u>indissolubility</u> of that which God joins together, no man can separate.

Marriage, the way God intended, is a mystery. He says you become one—not two and symbolically one—rather, "one flesh," no longer independent of each other. A harmonious union—as the left hand works in union with the right hand. Corinthians 7:4 states:

> **"A wife does not belong to herself but to her husband; equally a husband does not belong to himself but to his wife."**

Incredibly, "being one" is shown by God and the two parents participating together and procreating children. The child, genetically tied to both parents who are not genetically tied themselves, is the physical sign of their oneness. Children are the "physical manifestation" of a couple's oneness, thereby physically defining God's mystical uniting of a marriage as indissoluble as trying to undo a born child. Clearly stated, no valid marriage, blessed by God, can be undone by man. It is not within man's right. This is not man's opinion but God's. His truths are absolute. The Old Testament tells us God hates divorce. The New Testament confirms the indissolubility of marriage many times. Why are the Scriptures and the Church so uncompromising on these truths? Ivan, the visionary of Medjugorje states: *"God respects the family so much that when Jesus took human nature in the womb of Mary, He chose to live in a family."*

Our Lady tells us that is it by the family the future fruits of Her plans will be realized:

May 1, 1986

"I wish that the fruits in the family be seen one day."

Our Lady tells us, through Ivan, that if each family would pray and fast, there would be peace in the world. Therefore, the loving family is the most powerful structure in the world, and by guiding it, the Scriptures and the Church protect this structure from satan's plans to extinguish it. Consequently, there can be no compromise. By breaking up marriages, through man's decisions based on feelings rather than truths, satan's plans perpetuate and his power increases. In the following interviews with Jan Connell from the book, The Visions of The Children, Ivan tells of satan's hatred of the family and his desire to destroy it.

Ivan: *The young suffer much. It is worse than a war. It ruins their life.*

Q. *Why is all this happening, Ivan?*

A. *Because satan is present in these situations. Look at his influence in family life. The Blessed Mother says you can see his power in the high divorce rate world wide.*

Q. *Is satan responsible for divorce?*

A. *Of course. Divorce is the product of sin. Sin is the result of strong temptation. Sin is the result of weakness.*

At least one party in a marriage has to sin to destroy a sacramental union. Wherever there is sin, there is satan.

Q. *That sounds like the age-old, divide-and-conquer theory of war, Ivan.*

A. *Yes, satan is very smart. He has a large intellect. He knows all our weaknesses.*

Q. *Can you give us an example of his influence in the family, Ivan?*

A. *Yes. Look at the responsibility of parents. Often they are so interested in material things, peer pressure among friends, or personal gratification in each other to the exclusion of children both born and unborn. God has placed upon parents the responsibility to help and guide the young. <u>The parents' "first job" is to provide a loving environment of respect in which the children can grow up.</u> Often there is little or no love between a husband and a wife. Often there is little respect. When that happens, the spirit of the children is sickened. Then satan has immense power in the family. Where there is great love of luxury, or ease, or prestige, or professional accomplishment, satan has much power.*

Q. *What does he do with that power, Ivan?*

A. *He wants to destroy love and peace. When he destroys the home, he gains eternal power over many lives.*

Indeed, satan gains power over many lives by destroying a family. A novelist once wrote:

"Each divorce is the death of a small civilization."

There is a constant struggle for the family: one is for the devil to separate and destroy it, and the other is for God to keep and preserve it.

The devil knows that if the family and its structure are destroyed, then towns and cities fall, then nations and the world will follow. The cause of all our problems today is the assault from satan and the failure of the family in allowing God to preserve it. One grown man reports that when he was in eighth grade, the nun told the class, *"I'd rather my parents be dead than divorced."* It made such an impact on him that he remembers it perfectly years later. Marriage had that kind of permanence because people back then derived their truth from the Scriptures and lived it. Today, however, basing everything on feelings, there is such a lack of commitment that people rationalize that it is better to separate when there are hard times. While this kind of statement can raise anger in many who see their situation as horrible, it must be addressed. The truth must be given, however difficult it may be. A college student relates about his parents' divorce nine years ago, *"I was confused and angry when my parents split up. And it still feels as if they stabbed me in the heart."* There are far, far too many divorces taking place, and many of them are by Christians. One might think this author does not understand.

However, one of Our Lady's messages makes a profoundly bold statement. Before reading the message it is important to understand the depth of the word, "cruel." Here in this country, we have a much softer meaning than in former Yugoslavia. They live a hard life. They were under harsh Turkish occupation for centuries. There, many of us would describe their life as cruel. Their normal way of treating animals would surprise people in this country. The war in 1994 in Bosnia was a window into the depths of their cruelty on both sides. At the same time, they are warm people, full of love and chosen by Our Lady. Nevertheless, the word, "cruel," for them would mean something severe, extremely harsh, compared to our use of the word, "cruel," which would in many instances appear to them as minor nuisances or, in some cases, even silly.

In 1981, Our Lady was asked a question regarding a woman who wanted to leave her husband. She said her husband was "cruel" to her. Our Lady answered:

"Let her remain close to him and accept her suffering. Jesus, Himself also suffered."

It's an incredible message in that not only does Our Lady uphold the marriage, but she says, **"stay close to him!"** Why does Our Lady do this? Is it possible that She desires this man's conversion through the sufferings of his wife.? The Scriptures show perhaps why Our Lady validates the need to stay with him. But why is it necessary to stay close to him? Several scholars attributed the following words directly to Peter, our first Pope. Other scholars say it is Peter's words from the early Christians. What is important is that they are "God's Words" now because they are now in Sacred Scripture.

> *"You married women must obey your husbands so that any of them who do not believe in the word of the Gospel may be won over apart from preaching through their wives' conduct. They have only to observe the reverent purity of your way of life. Let not theirs be the outward adornment of braiding the hair, or of wearing gold, or of putting on robes; but let it be the inner life of the heart, in the imperishableness of a quiet and gentle spirit, which is of great price in the sight of God. For after this manner in old times the holy women also who hoped in God adorned themselves, while being subject to their husbands. So Sara obeyed Abraham, calling him lord. You are daughters of hers when you do what is right and fear no disturbance."* 1 Peter 3:1–6

Perhaps the conversion of the man (about whom Our Lady said to stay close to him) is through God's grace in the hands of the wife and, without her, he may be eternally damned. Blessed Anne-Marie Taigi would cook her husband's meal, and if it was not warmed perfectly he would do things like go into a rage and turn the table upside down and go out and give her a few minutes to do it right and return. She suffered incredibly, but she was perfect in her reactions. After her death, through most bitter tears, it was her husband's testimony which was most convincing for her being considered for canonization along with <u>her whole family.</u> Would Anne-Marie's husband have converted if she had not persevered? So, for a Christian today, there must remain the spirit of commitment for the sake of ourselves, our spouses, our children, and Our Lady's plans. If it is a good situation, then bless God; if it is a bad one, then still bless God and do everything possible to convert your spouse by your commitment, witness, and purity whether it's for better or for worse. If it is "worse," it is not justification to divorce.

What about divorce on the grounds of adultery? Nowhere in the Old or New Testament does the Bible grant divorce on the grounds of adultery. The following letter may show God's wisdom for having such a decree. The following letter perhaps testifies to the "truth" why:

Dear Caritas Members,

Today, I'm feeling on top of the world, so to speak. I just celebrated my 60th birthday and my husband, a non-Catholic, presented me with a very large statue of our beloved Mother, Mary. To make a long story short, my marriage of 40 years was on the verge of ending last year at this time. (My husband was at the end of a five-year affair). I was on the verge of emotional collapse. I prayed more Rosaries than I could say, Chaplets of Mercy, Sacred Heart prayers. My hus-

*band is a new man, a new husband, and we are
a couple very much in love with each other and
very beholding to Our Lady for having saved
our marriage. I can't tell you the love I have for
Her and Her Son. The suffering, I offer to Jesus
to join with His on the cross. My husband is a
police captain. I feel he is getting closer to God,
and I pray everyday for him and our children to
feel what I do for Jesus and Mary. Thank God
for you people of Caritas of Birmingham, and I
pray God gives you everything you need for this
task Our Lady is leading you to. With Her, nothing is impossible. Just ask me.*

Many Blessings, Field Angel

There can never be divorce—only annulling of the vows, and
this has to be determined by Christ through His Church. It is
not man's decision. Also, incompatibility is hardly a reason
for divorce since compatibility is a basic Christian tenant. If
an annulment is granted, it simply states there exists no valid
marriage blessed by God. Even the Church does not have
the authority or power to annul a validly blessed marriage by
God. The Vatican has recently stated that those in the Church
have been far too liberal in granting annulments and ex-
pressed the intention of greatly reducing the numbers granted.
Anyone whose life may be threatened should seek out a good,
sound, orthodox priest for guidance, and if separation is necessary, dating and remarriage are not permitted since you are

married for life. Separation leaves the door open for reconciliation. This problem existed in a community started by St. Paul named Corinth. He wrote to them and said:

> *"To those now married, however, I give this command (though it is not mine; it is the Lord's): a wife must not separate from her husband. If she does separate, she must either remain single or become reconciled to him again. Similarly, a husband must not divorce his wife."* 1 Cor. 7:10–11

Mark was an interpreter for St. Peter. The New Testament also tells us of a John Mark who was Paul's associate. Peter's interpreter, Mark, and Paul's associate, John Mark, are considered by scholars to be the same man. That being the case, Mark's words would carry great weight since he spent a lot of time with both Peter and Paul—even greater because now they are absolute in God's Holy Book. Mark writes Jesus' words which state themselves nothing has changed since the very beginning:

> *"At the beginning of creation God made them male and female. For this reason a man shall leave his father and his mother and the two shall become as one. They are no longer two but one flesh. Therefore, let no man separate what God has joined together... Whoever divorces his wife and marries another, commits adultery against her; and the woman who di-*

vorces her husband and marries another, commits adultery." Mark 10:6–9, 11–12

A physician wrote to a friend, whom he referred in his letter as "a friend of God," the same words Mark used. The Doctor was a good friend of St. Paul and his name was Luke, and now you can find his words of Jesus's words in God's Word:

"Everyone who divorces his wife and marries another commits adultery. The man who marries a woman divorced from her husband likewise commits adultery." Luke 16:18

How strongly should these truths be held in our hearts? Jesus Himself tells us the significance of these words. To understand, ask yourself what an event it would be if the heavens and earth were to pass away. What could compare to this momentous event? Yet the verse immediately preceding the one just read quotes Jesus saying:

"It is easier for Heaven and earth to pass away than for a single stroke of the letter of the law to pass." Luke 16:17

These words of Jesus are profound. The fact that they appear in verse 17, just before the statement on divorce, is no coincidence. We must realize how imperishable are God's words — His truths. Then, who dares to go against them? In Matthew, the same words that Luke used (regarding divorce) appear with only a few words added:

"I now say to you, whoever divorces his wife, unless the marriage, is unlawful and marries another, commits adultery..." Matthew 19:9

Most scholars agree the "unless the marriage is unlawful" refers to Christians, who, prior to their conversions had married blood relatives. Once they became Christians and realized their marriages were invalid because of immorality of incest, it was the only legitimate cause for divorce. Matthew's exception cannot easily be interpreted to mean anything other than that, although many today want otherwise. It would be difficult to reconcile it with the accounts of Mark and Luke. Also from the beginning, the more stringent words of Jesus in Mark and Luke are what prevailed throughout the Church from the beginning.

It is satan's plan to deceive many, even Christians, and many, indeed, have been in a slumber only to wake up and realize they are in extremely difficult, tangled up situations. For many there will be suffering for the rest of their lives because of their situation. For those, it should be offered up as restitution and reparation. Those who have awakened and find themselves in a terrible situation must find a priest or holy person who will stand on truth and the guidance of the Church and help them as best as he can make their lives right according to God's precepts. That priest or person may be difficult to find because many today will tell people what they want to hear rather than stand up for what the Scriptures and the Church teaches. Our Lady has come to reconcile us to God. While many of us are in a bad situation either through our own fault or through no fault of our own, we must start "today"—immediately—reconciling back to God and living His precepts. Difficult as it may be, it will be no more difficult than what the early Christians had to endure in their conversion from paganism to Christianity. To dwell too much on the past or the future can overwhelm us and even lead to hopelessness. What is important is to start "today" to live a new life.

Our Lady is coming to strengthen the family, to remind it of its function and its responsibilities, especially through the parents. Children will change if parents change. Once we realize there is no dissolving a valid marriage, (again satan has deceived many who believe we can) then we can be taught by Our Lady how to protect the family, using the indissoluble vows as our foundation.

Just as Jesus constantly reflected deeply on the law and the Scriptures, Our Lady now comes and invites us to read the Scriptures, and go more deeply into Jesus' words. Jesus' words go beyond the physical act of adultery when He says:

> *"You have heard the commandment, you shall not commit adultery. What I say to you is anyone who looks lustfully at a woman has already committed adultery in his heart."* Matthew 5:27–28

The point we wish to make is not the sin of adultery but its conception in the heart; and then, would the same spirit of truth apply to the sin of divorce when it is conceived in the heart? Every act of adultery starts in the heart where it is conceived. But Christians say, *"I would never commit adultery."* What of Christian couples who are married, going in two different directions, living together in the same house but apart in their hearts? Does not the spirit of truth in Jesus' words also apply to those who daily chip and gnaw at their marriage vows by having separation in their heart? A major factor in husbands' and wives' separating themselves in their hearts is society's powerful movement to restructure the authority in the families. Our Lady's messages now make us see this is so. An absolute truth is Malachi 2:16:

"For I hate divorce, says the Lord God of Israel."

If God hates divorce, does He not also hate the "action" of the breaking of the union in couples' hearts? It is as Ivan says, *"Parents have too much love of life and things than each other."* Without the proper order of authority in family, it is very difficult for it to function as God intended. This may be best explained by the following story.

There were three men. Each had a dominant right hand which could communicate with the left hand. The first man's hands did many successful jobs, working quietly together, making their tasks fruitful. Many times the dominant hand did a job it alone could do better than the other, such as pitching a ball. But it could not do it alone and its success depended on the left hand to catch it and then give the ball to the other hand which it alone could do better than the right hand. So, success of the pitch was a credit to both of their united and harmonious efforts. The dominant hand was humble enough to always give credit to the left hand, knowing its success depended on the other and the left hand was humble enough to give way to the dominant right hand to do its best. Both knew so well their roles and supported each other that they accomplished everything they set out to do, nearly perfectly.

The second man's set of hands were different. One day the less dominant hand said to the other, *"I want to pitch."* The dominant hand hesitated and thought, *"Well, okay."* So the left hand began to pitch. It was awkward. Meanwhile, the dominant hand was not accustomed to catching the ball and was not able to do it as well as the left hand. The left hand tried to pitch the ball and almost never got it near the plate. Sometimes it would even injure the batter, so awkward was its pitch because of trying to do something it was not able to do.

When it was time for the third man's dominant hand to pitch, the left hand said it wanted to pitch. The right hand, knowing it could do much better, said, *"NO."* The left hand then said it was going to pitch anyway and the right hand said, *"No, I know better how to do it and it is my duty."* This erupted into a fight with both unable to catch or pitch, much less get any ball even in the direction of the plate.

All three of the above describes the working relationship of husbands and wives. The first example shows one that is beautiful and harmonious, working as one as God intended. They did everything well with sound established rules and balance. At every attempt, together they produced and accomplished every goal set before them. The second shows where authority is confused; the wife taking a role that should be the husband's and the husband taking that of the wife's. They try to make it work but endure many failures, and they will meet with few successes unlike the first example. The third is a husband who understands what he is supposed to do, but the wife wishes not to submit to him and to his right to do so. Anarchy sets in and total disfunction of the family ensues. The children of all three are a reflection of their parents, having been taught by them through their example. The children of the first family reflected peace; the second, confusion; the third, war.

How does the above apply to the family? What is the family? How is it supposed to function? What are the truths about the family? The Bible tells us a great deal about how the family is suppose to work. Our Lady's messages also do. The vows of love and commitment are its foundation. Today families many times act independently of each other, democratically, with no real order or clear authority. Ivan said authority was to be respected in the family. Marija in 1987 told a group of 25 married couples that every family was to become holy and is like a little church. The father in the family is like the Heavenly Father, guiding and loving His Church. In Marija's own simple words, she revealed a truth that the Bible clearly confirms—that a husband, father, must love his wife above all, caring for her and their children and guiding them as Christ is the head of His Church and guides it. William Barclay said:

> *"We can never afford to forget that we teach our children to call God, Father, and the only conception of fatherhood that they can have is the conception which we give them. Human fatherhood should be molded and modeled on the pattern of the fatherhood of God. It is a tremendous duty of the human father to be as good a father as God."*

In today's family, the structure is confused and rarely based on how the Bible has shown us. Many don't want the truth and have arranged the structure of their family on what society has dictated and what they **feel**. Yet God shows us in His Book of Truth that He even respects his own order of authority. Mary is Queen of the angels. She is more deserving than all angels, all prophets, and all men put together. It is befitting that the Angel Gabriel came to Her during the Annunciation. Yet something happened once She married Joseph. While he is important, his role is not of the magnitude of Mary's and yet, when they married, God respects His own structure of the family so much that the angels appears not to Mary, who was more deserving, but to the lowly Joseph and tells him to take the Child and Mother and flee to Egypt. This drastically contrasts with today's society and its way of thinking. But can anyone really imagine Mary saying, *"Wait a minute, Joseph, I'm the Virgin Mary. Why didn't the angel appear to me? How do you know what you're doing is right? Remember, I am full of* *wisdom. Joseph, Joseph, Joseph… I'm not sure its God's Will."* No. Mary totally submitted herself to her husband's guidance because She knew it represented the Father's.

Many today try to change this truth, saying, *"That was 2,000 years ago,"* or *"Man and wife are subject to each other."* Others feel we must do what our conscience tells us. Still others overrule their husbands, or some husbands even become subject to their wives. We are a modern society with modern ideals, not antiquated ones. Yet this modern society has a host of problems as never before, and could it possibly be that the structure of today's family may not be correct?

Today's society has no problems with having positions like the following: pilot and co-pilot, president and vice president, head coach and assistant coach, manager and assistant manager, etc. Society knows that to have it otherwise would bring disorder, then anarchy. Suppose the airline co-pilot decides he would make decisions reserved only for the pilot. For the pilot to repeatedly contest would eventually lead to breakdown of order and lack of respect for his authority. But for both to work together in harmony, respecting each other's position and role, will result in everything going smoothly. Mary, who was greater, subjected Herself to that order of authority. The Scriptures tell us that all authority comes from God. God has ordained through the Scriptures that those who follow it will not be led to domination, making others their slaves, but to freedom. When a father or mother both do not fulfill this obligation, society becomes diseased. This problem now is a major factor in the deterioration of our society. How? When a husband loves, cares, guides and provides for his wife, he teaches his children and everyone else to do the same. When a wife's wants become her husbands wants, as Scripture states, when she respects, obeys, and pleases him, it will teach their children to do the same. They, in turn, will act accordingly toward their mother and the family will be one! Children are taught how to care for those who cannot care for themselves through the father who cares for the family he has been given who is dependent on him. Children will respect policemen, teachers, and others and their authority when a wife respects the authority of her husband and follows his guidance. The two parents fulfilling their scriptural roles make a completeness, a wholeness. This creates an environment so stable for children that there is no need for anything else. When a wife treats her husband as a king, she establishes herself as a queen because where there is a king, there is a queen. The children become royal members of the court. Through authority, love will **"reign"** in this little kingdom, and it will become, through the authority of God the Father, through the authority of the husband, and through the authority of the wife, the reign of love.

Ivan states after responding to the following question, *"What about parental authority?"* Many young people rebel against their parents' ways. Does the Blessed Mother speak about that?

van: *"The 'authority' of parents is a 'regime' of love. What kind of freedom do we give youth? Where is satan?*

Do parents really help satan by neglecting their duties? Their authority? Parents must restrict their own freedom in service to their children, just as children must obey and love their parents. Sacrificial love brings great blessings for parents and children."

Real love will never be where authority can't be. Where there is respect and authority, there you will find fertile ground for love and for it to grow.

We might think, *"This would be beautiful if both parents fulfilled this, but my spouse will never live this way."* Or, *"I wish my spouse would do this."* We have to look at ourselves and, regardless of our spouses faults, strive to live a perfect Christian life. One husband wrote that after his wife would not follow his guidance for his children and flatly refused to obey, he told her:

> *"It is your choice to go against me in this manner. But I base my beliefs of having the authority and right to lead my family in the direction we are going as the same right Jesus has in directing and leading His Church, and as husband and father, I will not relinquish my right, however determined you are against me."*

A wife, for her part, should stand also on truth following the Scriptures perfectly even if the husband will not fulfill his role. She, according to Scriptures, is to be saved through motherhood, childbirth, not sitting in a board room or performing social trivialities as society wishes to dictate to us. The Bible guides us on in truth.

> *"Moreover, it was not Adam who was deceived, but the woman. It is she who was led astray and fell into sin. She will be saved through childbearing, provided she continues in faith and love and holiness."* 1 Timothy 2:14–15

Is it coincidental that families flourished when the spirit of the Scriptures were followed and now that it is not, families are struggling and even dying?

A wife might think, *"My husband can't nail a board. I'm not going to let him guide my family!"* A husband who prays, who really wants to do right, will be inspired as a father by the Father what to do and what paths to travel. If done in good will and intent, God will even make his mistakes fruitful. Even if a husband does not want to be a good husband and father, a wife is not exempt from what Scripture teaches any more than a husband is exempt from his role because his wife is not a good spouse. A verse in Scripture which chokes many, and others simply wish to ignore states:

> *"Wives should be submissive to their husbands as if to the Lord. Because the husband is a head of his wife just as Christ is head of his body the Church as well as its Savior. As the Church sub-*

mits to Christ, so wives should submit to their husbands in everything." Ephesians 5:22–24

Regarding marriage, the word, "submit" has been made by satan to mean slavery, when, in fact, God's truth shows us clearly it leads to freedom. When the husband submits to the Heavenly Father and God's precepts, when the wife submits to her husband, and when the children submit to their parents, a beautiful Divine Order exists, birthing and fostering peace and love. Many today don't want to hear the absolutes above from Ephesians. They wish to dismiss this truth, holding on to their worthless feelings and opinions. However one wishes to look at it, God's Word says what it says. It is interesting to note the verse states, "Christ is the head of His body, the Church." Where there is a body, there has to be a head. Our head tells the body what to do and keeps everything—legs, feet, arms, hands—moving in harmony and all as one, collectively, accomplishes even difficult tasks. The right hand cannot say to the head, *"I will not obey,"* or the left hand to the right, *"I want to do the job you are doing."* This would make for a dysfunctional body and, indeed, when disease sets in a body, a signal from the head tells a paralyzed leg to move and it won't, the whole body is hampered.

So when there is a straying from the truth, disease sets in on the family today who doesn't want truth but prefers flexible truth. They are not a harmonious unit but an independent unit; like unsynchronized gears breaking each other apart. But for those parents who understand this Scripture, their families are a nurturing place of love and they, together using God's precepts, are able to teach their children real love of God through their witness. Jelena, the innerlocutionist of Medjugorje, says some incredible words about the importance of how parents teach children love.

Jelena: *The Blessed Mother says God intended love and respect between parents and children. Then the relationship will be happy.*

Q: *How do the parents and children achieve this love and respect?*

A: *By watching and emulating the love and respect between the mother and father.*

Q: *But if there is no love and respect between husband and wife, this can poison future generations.*

A: *Without prayers, fasting, and sacrificial love by both mother and father, family harmony is impossible.*

Q: *What does the Blessed Mother say about family life where only one member prays, fasts, and sacrifices?*

A: *The lost family is one where no one sacrifices. The more members of a family who pray, fast, and sacrifice, the more peace and happiness the family experiences.*

Indeed, love is the most important lesson we can teach our children. It insures our future and that of society. Many saints have spoken of this type of love. Our Lady has told us to read the lives of the saints. One holy soul has claimed that Jesus revealed to her that though He lived in poverty, He had everything. She states Jesus said:

> *"Not even now that I am in Heaven can I forget the happy hours I spent beside Joseph who, as if he were playing with Me, guided Me to the point of being capable of working. And when I look at My putative father, I see once again the little kitchen garden and the smoky workshop, and I still appear to see Mother peep in with Her beautiful smile which turned the place into Paradise and made us so happy.*

> *"How much families should learn from the perfection of this couple who loved each other as nobody else ever loved! Joseph was the head of the family, and as such, his authority was undisputed and indisputable: before it the Spouse and Mother of God bent reverently and the Son of God submitted Himself willingly. Whatever Joseph decided to do, was well done: there were no discussions, no punctiliousness, no opposition. His word was our little law. And yet, how much humility there was in him! There was never any abuse of power, or any decision against reason only because he was the head of the family. His Spouse was his sweet adviser. And if in Her deep*

humility She considered Herself the servant of Her consort, he drew from Her wisdom of Full of Grace, light to guide him in all events.

"And I grew like a flower protected by vigorous trees, between those two loves that interlaced above Me, to protect Me, and love Me.

"No. As long as I was able to ignore the world because of My age, I did not regret being absent from Paradise. God the Father and the Holy Spirit were not absent, because Mary was full of Them. And the angels dwelt there, because nothing drove them away from that house. And one of them, I might say, had become flesh and was Joseph, an angelical soul freed from the burden of the flesh, intent only on serving God and His cause and loving Him as the Seraphim love Him. Joseph's look! It was as placid and pure as the brightness of a star unaware of worldly concupiscence. It was peace, and our strength.

"Many think that I did not suffer as a human being when the holy glance of the guardian of our home was extinguished by death. If I was God, and as such I was aware of the happy destiny of Joseph, and consequently I was not sorry for his death, because after, a short time in Limbo, I was going to open Heaven to him, as a Man I cried bitterly in the

house now empty and deprived of his presence. I
cried over My dead friend, and should I not have
cried over My holy friend, on whose chest I had
slept when I was a little boy, and from whom I had
received so much love in so many years?

"Finally I would like to draw the attention of
parents to how Joseph made a clever workman of
Me, without any help of pedagogical learning. As
soon as I was old enough to handle tools, he did
not let Me lead a life of idleness, but he started me
to work and he made use of My love for Mary
as the means to spur Me to work. I was to make
useful things for Mother. That is how he incul-
cated the respect which every son should have
for his mother and the teaching for the future
carpenter was based on that respectful and loving
incentive.

"Where are now the families in which the little
ones are taught to love and work as a means of
pleasing their parents? Children, nowadays, are
the tyrants of the house. They grow hard, indif-
ferent, ill-mannered towards their parents. They
consider their parents as their servants, their
slaves. They do not love their parents and they
are scarcely loved by them. The "reason" is that
while you allow you children to become objec-

tionable, overbearing fellows, you become de-
tached from them with shameful indifference.

"They are everybody's children, except yours,
o parents of the twentieth century. They are the
children of the nurse, of the governess, of the col-
lege, if you are rich people. They belong to their
companion they are the children of the streets,
of the schools, if you are poor. But they are not
yours. You, mothers, give birth to them and that
is all. And you, fathers, do exactly the same. But
a son is not only flesh. He has a mind, a heart,
a soul. Believe Me, no one is more entitled and
more obliged than a father and a mother to form
that mind, that heart, that soul.

"A family is necessary: it exists and must ex-
ist. There is no theory or progress capable of
destroying this truth without causing ruin. A
shattered family can but yield men and women
who in future will be more perverted, and will
cause greater and greater ruin. And I tell you
most solemnly that it would be better if there
were no more marriages and no more children
on the earth, rather than have families less united
than the tribe of monkeys, families which are not
schools of virtue, of work, of love, of religion, but
a babel in which everyone lives on his own like
disengaged gears, which end up by breaking.

"Broken families. You break up the most holy way of social living and you see and suffer the consequences. You may continue thus, if you so wish. But do not complain if this world is becoming a deeper and deeper hell, a swelling place of monsters who devour families and nations.

Can any one deny the spirit of truth in the above? In regards to married couples: We have mothers working, taking children to daycare, so their family can have a bigger house rather than staying at home and living in a smaller one. Fathers follow interests and hobbies which not only take away family money, but their time as well. Even if they can afford them, are these husbands reflections of God the Father in doing so? What about mothers who are always taxiing their children, like nomads, just to do what everyone else is doing? And the fathers who come home and rather than looking at their children and giving them some attention, stare into a useless box emitting the day's gossip of the world. A loving family which is built on a reflection of the Holy Family makes up an immensely powerful force and satan will do his best to strangle it through useless treats, pleasures, selfishness, no love, etc. For a child to be balanced, whole, equipped to handle anything that might come along, only one thing is necessary in the home. It's love between the two parents—sacrificial love. They will not only feel its warmth and security but its ability to make them whole. It is the child's real delight and the longing of his little soul whether he is two years old or 16 years old. All a child needs to be whole is two parents who love each other. One woman, who was raised in Poland, related: *"When I was a child, we lived on a farm. I never got anything, even on Christmas. I never had even a doll in my childhood, but it was the happiest time of my life, with two loving parents, and we worked and not once do I remember being bored."*

Today children have shelves, closets, and T.V. rooms full of toys and yet you will hear them say, *"We're bored."* They have to have one high after another becoming so full they are no longer satisfied with anything. You could live in a home with dirt floors, poorer, with your children not being perfect. They might not be pretty, or so smart; they might have attention deficits, etc., but if they are raised in a environment of love it will make up for all their deficiencies. They will be whole. In this country we place blame on poverty and call it a sin. Poverty is not a problem where there is love. Ask anyone who has been through it, like the woman from Poland. The poverty we now suffer from is lack of truth clouded by the decision to live our lives, directing ourselves according to our own truths which will always lead to a void and longing for something more.

We have created a terribly materialistic situation looking for comfort, ease, escape, and now families are drowning while parents follow their miserable interests. The following is a true story of a child who now is grown, relating one example of a father who literally crushed the heart of his child.

"I was just 12 when my Boy Scout troop planned a father-son camp-out. I was thrilled and could

hardly wait to rush home and give my dad all the information. I wanted so much to show him all I'd learned in scouting, and I was so proud when he said he'd go with me.

"The Friday of the camp-out finally came, and I had all my gear out on the porch, ready to stuff it in his car the moment he arrived. We were to meet at the local school at 5 o'clock and car pool to the campground. But dad didn't get home until 7 p.m.

"I was frantic, but he explained how things had gone wrong at work and told me not to worry. We could still get up first thing in the morning and join the others. After all, we had a map. I was disappointed, of course, but I decided to make the best of it.

"First thing in the morning, I was up and had ev-erything in the car while it was still getting light, all ready for us to catch up with my friends and their fathers at the campground. He said we'd leave around 7 a.m., but he didn't get up until 9:30.

"When he saw me standing out front with the camping gear, he finally explained that he had a bad back and couldn't sleep on the ground. He hoped I'd understand and that I'd be a 'big boy' about it...but could I please get my things out of

his car? He had several commitments he had to keep.

"Just about the hardest thing I've ever done was to go to the car and take out my sleeping bag, cooking stove, pup tent and supplies. And then— while I was putting my stuff away and he thought I was out of sight—I watched my father walk out to the garage, sling his golf clubs over his shoulder, throw them into the trunk and drive away to keep his 'commitment.'

"That's when I realized my dad never meant to go with me to the camp-out."

—taken from Focus on the Family

What can be more devastating to a child than a dad breaking a promise? How have we done the same to our children in different circumstances? At a high school banquet, one father who heads up a multi-sports program which has become very successful through total consumption of his days and nights, was on stage thanking everyone. When he got to his wife, he said:

"And my wife—She is very understanding. I am never home and I want to thank her for her understanding."

This man is putting all his time, his life, into a deception. It looks as though it's important, but years down the road when he has severely damaged his sacramental union, how will that school program pick up the pieces of his family? Who will remember what he did? Even if he sees the error now, how does he escape the monster which he's built which consumes all his time? How many little hearts have been broken in today's society that now only the Almighty, True Father will be able to heal. Our Lady goes so far as to tell us we are only interested in our miserable interests.

March 25, 1992

"Dear children, today as never before I invite you to live my messages and put them into practice in your life. I have come to help you and therefore I invite you to change your life because you have taken a path of misery, a path of ruin. When I told you, 'convert, pray, fast, be reconciled,' you took these messages superficially. You started to live them and then you stopped, because it was difficult for you. No, dear children, when something is good, you have to persevere in the good, and not think, 'God does not see me, He is not listening, He is not helping.' And so you have gone away from God and from Me because of your miserable interest. I wanted to create of you an oasis of peace, love, and goodness. God wanted you with your love and with His help to do miracles and thus give an example. Therefore, here is what I say to you, satan is playing with

you and with your souls and I cannot help you because you are far from My heart. Therefore, pray, live My messages and then you will see the miracles of God's love in your everyday life. Thank you for having responded to my call."

This message is not being addressed to those in darkness but rather to us who are Christians and to those who will convert in the future. How can we tell those in darkness anything when wc ourselves are diseased by the world? Ivan states:

Q: *You often speak of the disease of materialism. What is that disease? What are the symptoms?*

A: *Materialism is a sickness. Things become more important than they really are. There is kind of awareness blindness and people attach great importance to certain people or objects, like cars, houses, professional positions, or social positions. These become proportionally bigger and bigger until they eat up a person's whole sense of awareness. When that happens, love and peace and joy are no longer possible. Whole segments of the population of this planet are suffering from this illness. People's bellies have grown bloated with things as they die of hunger.*

Q: *Why?*

A: *Because the deepest longing of the human heart is God, not things. The solution to this illness is prayer with the heart, and fasting. If each family would pray and fast as a family, there would be peace in the world. If parents would pray, bless, and sacrifice more for their children, the children would thrive. If children would pray for their parents, especially for the safety of their parents' marriage, and love and obey their parents, family life would be a source of great love and peace on earth. God's abundance would fill the homes. Where there is no prayer and sacrifice, God is absent. A place without God is a place of great danger and pain. Family prayer and penance will bring peace in people, peace in the Church, and peace in the world.*

The only way we can help is through family prayer. The family is greatly threatened now by the disease of materialism. We work, have pleasures, sports, etc., therefore, we have no time to pray together.

This is the great excuse, but it's really a great lie; "most" people are living this lie. The Blessed Mother has promised that for families who pray together there will be harmony and unity. It must begin when children are babies. By the time children are in their twenties, it is very hard to erase bad habits they have acquired.

Indeed our families today are completely absorbed by material things. We spend a great deal of time just keeping up cars, homes, and so many things and also activities which appear useful yet keep us enslaved to the point where there is no time to even "think" and "reason" where and what we really should be doing. Our Lady said:

January 25, 1989

"Pray because you are in great temptation and danger because the world and material goods lead you into slavery. satan is active in this plan."

One mother, after watching their Christmas film of their three year old, ten years after it was taken, was shocked at it herself. She states:

"On film I saw myself and my three year old come down the steps and then stand before his toys without any excitement. I watched myself pick up toys and act excited, saying, 'Wee, wee;' then I picked up another toy trying to gleam and show him he should be excited. As I watched I became sickened with myself. He just stood there and could care less. What I didn't know then and what I know now through prayer is I've taught my children to want, to desire, to possess, all to my family's detriment. I wish I had known then what I know now. I've opened doors which I cannot easily or perhaps ever shut, and materialism is now in my children's hearts."

Indeed many children who are really pure have been led to impurity, even by their own parents. The price we pay for it is the loss of God in our lives. Things replace God.

A holy soul who died in 1961 and whose work is being accepted all over the world, relayed words of Jesus that she claims He told her about this impurity we place in our children:

"God does not stay with the impure. Because impurity corrupts what is the property of God: souls, and in particular the souls of children who are angels spread over the earth. Woe to those who tear off their wings with the cruelty of devilish beasts and throw these flowers of Heaven into the moor, by letting them taste the flavor of material things! Woe... It would be better if they died struck by thunderbolts rather than commit such sin!

"Woe to you, rich and fast living people! Because it is amongst you that the greatest impurity thrives and idleness and money are its bed and pillow! You are now sated. The food of concupiscence reaches your throats and chokes you. But you will be hungry. And your hunger will be terrible, insatiable and unappeasable forever and ever. You are now rich. How much good you could do with your wealth! Instead you do so much harm both to yourselves and to other people. But you will experience a dreadful poverty on a day that will have no end. You now laugh (at your socials; your frivolous merry making and lives)."

Not to exclude those who are even more responsible, what of those marriages of men and women where one spouse is perfect? What does the loving Father look down and see? How He must be deeply saddened to see the man going off preoccupied with his golf games or other pleasures, his vacation, his retirement, all the while the spouse reacts to him perfectly, never criticizing, never demanding but wishing—O how the spouse desires passionately for him to be a better husband. What of those wives whose spouse is perfect, who, following their own agendas, disregard what their spouse wishes? They draw themselves and contaminate themselves in the world by its preoccupation, all the while their spouse desires to lead them to a better way. And even of the religious vocation, what sort of sad judgement awaits those who have committed infidelity against a perfect spouse, so perfect that he had them drawn to his heart through the pure fire of their hearts; of hearing his proposal to become His bride as priests and nuns? How many wrongs have been committed against the pure One, against those vows made to Jesus which are sealed in His heart forever? Yet, there are so many who violate their vows from one day to the next. All of us, in some way, are wed to the pure One and we offend Him by not submitting to His desires, His Church, and His authority. This is indeed a grave matter which affects the whole family of the Church.

Because of the lack of truth in Christian lives, the world situation is grave. It is Our Lady who says, "I've come because faith is extinguishing itself."

Spring 1982

> **"…My children, have you not observed that
> faith began to extinguish itself? There are
> many who do not come to church except
> through habit…"**

To whom is She talking about "the Faith?" It is to us
Christians—children, singles, married couples, priests, nuns,
widowed. To us in the Christian Church who are in crisis. To
us who represent "the Faith," and who point the finger at
those in darkness, ignoring the three fingers pointing back at
us. We are three times more responsible than that one person
who is n darkness. How can he become light if we do not live
light? For thirty* years…..everyday…..thirty long years…..
Heaven is so desperate to reach us that it is speaking to us as
never before in the history of the world. And now it is twenty-
eight years of apparitions! Our Lady said:

April 4, 1985

> **"…I wish to keep on giving you messages as it
> has never been in history from the beginning of
> the world."**

Our Lady has said, **"God 'tells' me what to convey in
these messages to the world."** God conveys through Mary a

---

* This was originally written in 1993. We only updated the year in our reprinting. Often many of
these writings are foreseen, even prophetic, by realizing when it was originally written— which
the update could make you think it was written in hindsight rather than foresight.

chilling, "awakening" message about Her (after these apparitions):

May 2, 1982

"I will not appear anymore on this earth."

These "three" things have never happened in Church history before:

1. Messages given by Our Lady as never before in history.
2. Apparitions from Our Lady on a daily basis for 30 years.
3. Our Lady has said these are Her last apparitions on earth.

These three fingers indict us just as three fingers pointing back at us when we point a finger would. They impel us to live God's Commandments, to live His truth. His truths today are calling out to fathers to live your roles, to stand through love on truth and lead your family to the Promised Land and start to teach the importance of spiritual success, not worldly success. A father must always remember every action of his is a lesson to his children and the Book of Proverbs announced this truth:

> *"My Son, pay attention to me and watch closely what I do."*

So fathers, watch the Father and live the proverb, so that our children will be perfect as the Father is perfect. If George Herbert, who said: *"One father is more than one hundred school masters,"* words are true, then Herman Beeches' words ring true when he said, *"The mother's heart is the child's school-room,"* and still even more true are the words of Pope Paul VI, reflecting the Scriptures of a mother's quite hidden role when he says, *"Every mother is like Moses... she doesn't enter the Promised Land. She prepares a world she will not see."*

Fathers are to lead to the Promised Land those whom the mothers prepare to go there! James Dobson says, *"I believe successful families begin with the father."* That is based on Scripture. Then Scripture shows us it is the mother who make the family work. So the successful family begins with the father and ends with the mother. But at the same time, "both" the beginning and the end come through the mother. Families are here to be dwelling places for the raising of saints, a school where children are taught that it is through holiness that they will gain everything. Just as a baby is birthed through the Mother, now Our Lady tells us She wishes to birth us into Holiness.

March 25, 1990

> **"...As I bore Jesus in my womb, so also, dear children, do I wish to bear you unto holiness..."**

Motherhood is a sacred calling and, when it's done with a desire for perfection, its fruits impact the world. For those who want truth, it is God the Father leading us through Mary, the Mother, to radically change our lives and not go in the direction of society which de-emphasizes the importance of our roles but rather to elevate motherhood and respect and live up to fatherhood. Mothers must realize that through them they impact and change the whole world, for every boy and every girl comes through them. A mother cheats and deprives herself of making a strong, lasting mark on the world when she sits in an office or board room as one voice when she could be raising several who would carry her voice in board rooms, families, and a host of other places, through which holy influence will alter society and, thereby, the world. It is not just working mothers but also those roles of wife and mother that Our Lady, through the guideship* of the Father, calls us back. Mary incredibly makes a statement about how important motherhood is by excluding all but mothers in a blessing in which She plainly singles out mothers. She even did something you rarely see Our Lady do. She told them six days beforehand what She was going to do as if to further emphasize it.

December 19, 1985

> **"I wish in a special way on Christmas Day to give mothers my own special motherly blessing and Jesus will bless the rest with His own blessing."**

Following Our Lady's messages, it has become quite evident that it is through Her as a mother that motherhood will heal the world. Our Lady submits completely to the Fa-

---

* Guideship: literally the lead "ship" to follow to safety, especially during storms. Families who understand this will always be led through the errors and storms of society to safe harbors by God the Father inspiring fathers.

ther's guideship, giving good example to all married couples. It is through His authority that She guides us as children of God. It is emphasized in every message, "dear children," and sometimes Our Lady even calls us "little children." It is a big statement that She is re-establishing the family—She, the Mother; God, the Father; we, their children—that earthly mothers, fathers and children will know how to function as a sacred structure of authority where love reigns.

In the future, as society heads toward total disaster, whose children do you want to be? Children of the world or children of Mary? Whose Son was Jesus, thereby making Him our Brother? Whose Father was God, thereby making Him also our loving Father? How sad it is for those who neither want to be in this family, nor wish their own family to reflect that sacred oneness. That oneness of our Heavenly Mother and our Heavenly Father is the outline and example on which all families should structure themselves to work. It offers the best protection from satan.

After reading all the preceding, it may be understandable how one could be deeply hurt, wounded, and lacerated in the heart by God's truth; yet sometimes this may be exactly what's needed to reconcile ourselves back to God as His people. There is no desire to condemn anyone, whether it be someone who has divorced and remarried, the married couple who are living divorce within their marriage, or the priest or nun fulfilling their role without the spirit of being truly married to the Master. These words are written to all of us to stop in our tracks; to elevate us to "reason" out the "truth;" to reconcile everything in our lives which stands on untruth; to match up our lives with the Scriptures, the Church, the lives of the saints, and live a truly free and real life, a life of peace, knowing all areas of our lives are reconciled to God. There is no greater security especially in a society which is uncertain and offers no security. We do not condemn those in situations that have caused you to live in sin whether through your own fault or not. We repeat what Jesus said to the adulteress after the pharisees left:

> ***"Who condemns you? Then neither do I condemn you. Go and sin no more."*** John 8:10–11

We have to live Jesus' words. The woman was living in sin but Jesus' message to her was: NOW, from today, go and sin no more. Our Lady says the same to us through Her messages when over, and over She starts Her monthly messages with the words, "today." Just as Jesus knows, She knows we've been living in sin and knows God is willing to forgive us, but from this day forward, She tells us to sin no more and start living a new life. If these writings convict you of the wrongs you have done, they are not intended to condemn you or your past; rather, they are intended to alert you that **"today"** is the time to change and live the truth.

If we do what God wants and not what we want, peace settles in our families. The world will then know peace. We know our Savior was born in the midst of cold, in a stable, dreary by all standards by which the world measures, but warmed with the fire of Mary and Joseph's love. What else could be needed for the little Savior? He had everything that night because God, a good Father, saw to it. Jesus had the best—the love of Mary and Joseph. Nothing more could have been given. We think we give our children a lot when we give them things, education, pleasures—but how little we give them by comparison to what Mary and Joseph gave and they had none of the things we give. Let this Christmas* be different. Let Christmas be full of tears of repentance and sorrow so deep that nothing else will be left to fill it except joy. Give God your heart this Christmas and spend it in the only way it should be spent—in love—sacrificial love. Recommit yourself to your spouse, thereby enveloping and giving love to your family this Christmas.

December 25, 1992

> **"Dear children, today I wish to place you all under my mantle to protect you from every satanic attack. Today is the day of peace, but throughout the world there is much lack of peace. Therefore, I call you to build up a new world of peace together with me, by means of prayer. Without you, I cannot do that, and, therefore, I call all of you, with my motherly love, and God will do the rest. Therefore, open yourselves to God's plans and purposes for you to be able to cooperate with**

* These writings were originally printed in the July/December 1993 Caritas Newsletter for the Christmas edition.

Him for peace and for good. And do not forget that your life does not belong to you, but is a gift with which you must bring joy to others and lead them to eternal life. May the tenderness of little Jesus always accompany you. Thank you for having responded to my call.

The truths about what you have just read must be heard throughout the land, from families to the pulpits, from school teachers to businessmen in every occupation. All of us in society have made it too easy for families to break up. Support groups, equal pay for women, day care centers all seem to be the fair and equitable things to provide, but again satan has used our compassion to an extreme and has literally paved the way for husbands and wives to split up. Where is the support for the family? How many families would be together if there were extremely limited resources for husbands and wives to make it outside the family structure as was the situation 50 years ago? How many wives stayed with husbands because they knew they could never support themselves and their children without their husbands? And in the end, many marriages improved.* How much better did the children fare because society's pressure kept families intact? It is time we radically reevaluate many things that seemed right but now have proven wrong. The incentives to separate must be discouraged. We must teach our children these traditional values, based on

---

Recent statics show a high percentage of husbands and wives who stick it out, are happy five years past the crisis.

these truths, so that once again society will put motherhood on a pedestal as the most respected profession and honor it as no other occupation. For women to shun motherhood to pursue worldly occupations and attachments should be held by Christians in a negative view. While President Bush was in office, his wife, Barbara Bush, made a statement saying that what was most important in the long run was how good a wife and mother she was. Fifty years ago, women had their hearts based on truth. It was not a question of whether they could do a job as well as a man. Many women proved they could during World War II, moving into factories and doing men's work just as well, yet these women knew their God-given role. Regarding these women who filled the positions vacated by our servicemen during World War II, "The Cincinnati Enquirer" recently reprinted one of their articles from 1943:

> *"The women were said to 'look forward to the day when they could be relieved of these duties by the men and devote their time to the career they desire most—marriage and making a home.'"*

What about men? If the above is followed, then there will be better husbands because the mothers raising these little boys will see to it. When little boys are taught to love their mothers, they, in turn, will respect and love their future wives. Few today raise these issues for fear of hurting all those who have divorced and even remarried or who shun their role in pursuit of "self," or their own interests. We all make mistakes and no one needs to single out any individual for a wrong.

But we must start declaring through all of Christendom that the day has come to start living God's Commandments and teach this to everyone. Our Lady said:

January 25, 1987

> **"...Today I want to call you to start living a new life as of today..."**

For all those who feel out in the cold because of your families' tragedies, take heart and decide for God and go from this day forward and live His Commandments. If satan has trapped you in your situation and you can see no way out, take courage and remember Our Lady's message:

July 25, 1988

> **"Dear children, today I am calling you to a complete surrender to God. Everything you do and everything you possess give over to God so that He can take control in your life as King of all you possess. That way, through Me, God can lead you into the depths of the spiritual life. Little children, do not be afraid because I am with you even when you think that there is no way out and that satan is in control. I am bringing peace to you. I am your Mother and the Queen of Peace. I am blessing you with the blessing of joy so that for you God may be everything in life. Thank you for having responded to my call."**

No matter how impossible your situation may be, know there is a way out. But you must know clearly that if you do not start living God's Commandments, there is no hope for you because even the all-compassionate Mother will not be able to help you. On October 25, 1993, Our Lady said:

"I cannot help you if you do not live God's Commandments, if you do not live the Mass, if you do not abandon sin…"

For those who read these pages, you already have our* prayers for you to bear the truth. We will pray for you. We end as we began. To all of you who are our brothers, we greet you with truth. May it wipe away your darkness and fill you with the light and may the light bring peace to you. Decide for God. We send you our love.

* * * * * * * * * * * *

We are receiving thousands of letters about the articles which you have just read, originally printed in July/December, 1993 Caritas Newsletter. Within four weeks of its distribution, we heard from eight people whose marriages were headed for divorce but have changed their minds. Hundreds of families are writing saying they are being healed and are beginning the path of getting their lives in harmony with God. This is resulting in many experiencing peace in spite of difficult situations.

---

* Referring to the Community of Caritas.

The following are just a few of the letters we have received about the effects these truths are having on people's lives:

Dear Caritas,

Please send me your newsletter for my mother (from Kansas) mailed me her copy and I read it. I need help from God. I wish to turn my life around before it is too late. I am 42 and live alone. I am divorced and wronged my wife and family. I just hope God can forgive me for the sins I have lived the past twenty years. I would like a few copies of "The Painful Truth."

Sincerely Yours,
Swanton, Ohio

Dear Caritas,   *December 3, 1993*

God bless you. This last newsletter really hit home for me and I hope to distribute it to others. When I strayed from the Catholic Church many years ago, I led my husband and two children with me. I am back now and my husband seems to be heading in the right direction thanks to our Mother's intercession; but my children are grown and have moved away. I have very little influence over them anymore. I have much remorse but also much confidence in God's mercy. I know that through my prayer, fasting, and sacrifice, all three of them will be given the gift of Faith once more. God is so good. His Mother is a great help.

That is why this issue is so special. I know of many homes that need Mary's intercession. I attend daily Mass at different churches and I'll put a few copies in each one. Times like this, I wish I had a job so I could send you a nice big donation, but I can still pray for you. My order form is enclosed with my small donation.

Yours in Christ,
Altoona, Pennsylvania

Dear Caritas,   *January 3, 1994*

I just want to say just how very much I enjoyed reading your newsletter and to say, "Thank you."

My husband, Gerald, and I have been married for almost 19 years and we have three beautiful children but we are separated. For about two and a half years now, the kids and I have bombarded Heaven with rosaries, chaplets of Mercy, novenas and prayers asking God to heal and restore our marriage and family. My husband says that he wants to come home but he can't seem to take that final step to come back and make a commitment to me and our marriage. Many times I've been greatly tempted to just give up and get on with my life, but I've never been able to let go of the hope that God would heal and restore my marriage and our family. Anyway, your last newsletter (July through December, 1993) was a very special one to me because it reaffirms what marriage means to me and also reaffirms my hope. Thanks a lot and God bless you.

> *Sincerely,*
> *New Iberia, Loisiana*

My Beautiful Devotees of Mary, Jesus' Mother,

The newsletter just received (July through December) is a masterpiece <u>and</u> mouthpiece of our Holy Father <u>and </u>the Holy Spirit concerning family life. Each word was issued through the inspiration of the Holy Spirit. I beg you to send 200 copies of this newsletter for distribution. May God reward you. Enclosed is for postage—my last dollars. Sorry it isn't more. Will donate after we receive gifts.

> *Love and Joy in Jesus and Mary,*
> *A nun from Braddock, Pennsylvani*

Dear Friends,

want to tell you that your last newsletter was a very great blessing to me. I did as you asked, and prayed to the Holy Spirit and discovered myself in your description of what is wrong with marriages in today's society. I discovered that I have been living as though divorced from my husband. It opened my eyes to some negative attitudes that have been developing for several years and harming my marriage. I feel this was an inspired teaching and that many people will be blessed through it. My gratitude to Our Lady, the Beloved Holy Spirit, and to all of you for your dedication and devotion to your calling.

Yours in Jesus and Mary,
Dallas, Texas

Dear Caritas: January 25, 1994

have always enjoyed reading the messages of Mary through your newsletter, but your July–Dec, 1993 newsletter was the most inspirational I've read in such a long time. It has caused me to take a good, hard look at my own life with clear eyes, and there will be many positive changes as a result. Thank you for your straight-to-the-point article which has lifted the grey clouds of confusion which make it difficult to see what is right and what is not. Thank you and congratulations for having the courage to speak the truth in a time when it is so unfashionable to do so. I am forwarding my copy of the newsletter to someone else who desperately needs to hear its words. I hope they will have the same positive effect when they are read once more. The donation enclosed is for the additional printing of the article, "Whose Opinion is Right?"

Sincerely,
Highland, Illinios

Dear Caritas of Birmingham,   February 6, 1994

was given your newsletter by a friend. She gave it to me because my family has been going through some very tough times. My husband left eighteen months ago for another woman, after seventeen years of a wonderful marriage that has been blessed with three beautiful children. I have been trying to hold it together for my children and to keep our home running smoothly. It is very, very difficult. I don't want to give up on my husband or our marriage. We had everything beautiful in a family. Everyone who knows us, still shakes their head and says not you—you all were the perfect family. We were active in our church, our community, our children's schools and did family activities like ride bikes, walks, and dinner every night. We prayed together, but I know now we did not include enough prayer or praise of God in our lives.

I ask you to include my family and especially my husband in your community of prayer. We need so much help to turn this event in our lives around and with God's help, it can happen.

Your newsletter was such an inspiration to me. It gave me the hope that there is hope. It would be such an honor to be one of your "Field Angels." Thank you for entering my life at such a crucial time. God bless you and the work you do.

Sincerely,
Waldorf, Maryland

Dear Caritas of Birmingham,   February 8, 1994

I have a friend who receives your newsletters, and recently she passed me the one about "Whose Opinion is Right." She felt it had great meaning for our relationship (mine and my husband's).

We were married outside the Catholic Church because my husband is "divorced." I was widowed when we met; he had been separated a couple of years with no possibility of reconciliation. In our heart of hearts, I think we knew it was not right—but we could not accept the alternative. Then in 1991, we had the opportunity to travel to Medjugorje. I feel we had started

70

our conversion the year before, but Medjugorje made us start to pray more. We joined a weekly prayer group and change a lot in our lifestyle, such as no more TV, no more newspapers, magazines, etc. My husband quit drinking alcoholic beverages. We tried fasting on Wednesdays and Fridays. We don't always succeed, but we try. We attend Mass as often as possible, and we support more organizations like yourselves. This was basically Our Lady's miracles in our lives. However, the big day came when, on January 31, 1992, I had received a special blessing through Joseph Terelya. You may have heard of him. Anyway, I could not sleep that entire night. By morning, I had received a personal message, very strong, and I knew I must carry through with it. I was made to understand that I could no longer live as a wife to my husband. "It was wrong," is what I heard. So I cried a lot, not realizing that all would be okay, because it came from Our Blessed Mother. I worried how my husband would accept what I had to tell him. Well he took it as a relief, as if the weight of the world was removed from his shoulders. He had been feeling the same way, but did not know how to tell me. So you see, prayer and fasting does bring about great graces. We know! We are living proof. We have lived chaste lives since February 1, 1992.

Another story I would like to share with you is more painful but maybe you could use it somewhere, somehow. While I was growing up, I saw my father change from a very devoted family man, loving father, to an abusive violent alcoholic. My mother tells us this change lasted seven years. During these seven years, my mother prayed to God to cure him or to come and get him. My mother never entertained the though of leaving because she lived the way Our Blessed Mother asks all of us to live — She remained faithful to her husband even when she kept getting pregnant, she never refused him. We were a large family of 14 children. I was the fourth oldest and remember much of the good times and all of the bad times. Even today, my mother never speaks ill of my father, who, before he died had smashed my mother's head in with a hammer, nearly killing her. He died while running away from the scene. The police say he had passed out at the wheel and hit a rock cut.

I don't think women should have to suffer this much in our society, but my mother was the best model of living her vows "for better or for worse." She really truly "loved." She never bad mouthed my dad, but made us understand it was alcohol that made him this way. My mother is okay today. She lives a simple life. She is 65 years young and this incident happened when she was 36. With 14 children to care for, only my oldest sister had married by then and my one brother had been removed from the home because my dad used to beat him up for no reason when he would come home drunk. I know some of these things have left scars on my family, brothers and sisters. I pray they will all return to God for a real healing. I know my faith has helped pull me through many hard times.

Today, I thank God for all the people who are doing the right thing to bring people back to God. Some are harder to move than others. Their hearts are so hard because of the hurt they have suffered. I must trust in Our Blessed Mother's intervention and God's mercy. I pray for you all, and I ask that you pray for all of my family. These stories I shared with you because of the article, "Whose Opinion is Right."

Brothers and Sisters in Jesus Christ,
Meaford, Ontario, Canada

Dear Ones at Caritas,   *January 21, 1994*

Just writing to let you know how very powerful your last message of Our Lady (12/25/93) and your giving us the details and explanations was. When I told two of my daughters-in-law about it, all three of us were reduced to silence for quite a while. Praise God, and thanks to Our Lady for blessing you so richly! In these past two years, it's amazing how all the signs, hints, and messages point the very same way. I read Fr. Gobbi's locutions and Bud MacPhearson, Michael Brown, Miles Jeso, and my husband watches Jack Van Impe and Rush Limbaugh and everyone corroborates what you have told us <u>first</u>—Our Lady blesses you abundantly!

Also, your spirit-filled last newsletter—Thank God I did as you said and prayed very hard to the Holy Spirit on my knees beforehand—as it was, I about choked on it, and believe me, for two days I was not myself! If this much truth is so shocking, can you imagine what a mini-judgement would be like? No wonder some people might die to see themselves. But it was very salutary, and I'm going back to it again to try to take a little more truth.

Love in Jesus and Mary's Heart,
Lombard, Illinois

'What a wonderful edition (July–Dec. 1993). You opened my eyes as a father."

—Lake Oswego, Oregon

'I could never have been prepared for how much came to me from such a little article, or how much I would hurt from reading it. But it's a good hurt and something I'm glad for. Please send me 100 copies.

—Myrtle Beach, South Carolina

'Never have I read anything which made me understand my problems so clearly as the article the "Painful Truth."

—Boca Raton, Florida

'How is it there are thousands and thousands of counselors, organizations, education, etc., all over this land and your little articles, "Whose Opinion is Right/The Painful Truth," gives the answers, solid answers—not mush? I can't thank you enough, even though it hurts to read the truth."

—New Orleans, Loisiana

If Pulpits rang out the message in these writings, many problems would disappear!!

"You are right. I did almost choke when I read your articles. I know it took courage to say what you wrote. So many things are now clear. From reading your newsletter I am now challenged in a way that I know will change my whole family."

— Philadelphia, Pennsylvania

"Thousands who have read "Whose Opinion is Right/The Painful Truth" have also asked the questions: Who is directing the family? Where are we going? How will problems be fixed? This booklet is offered to you to open your eyes, leaving you with the thought that you know you will have to make decisions which will have a major impact on your life and those around you."

—Caritas of Birmingham

* * * * * * * * * * * *

A must read for every Christian. When you read it you'll know why people immediately start reading it a 2nd time and why others have read this book 5 times.

Readers agree this book will rank as one of the #1 books ever written connected to Medjugorje.

> "One of the most important books ever written."
>
> —C. H., Atlanta, Georgia

> "Your book really opened my eyes!!!"
>
> —J.P., Pittsburgh, Pennsylvania

> "How asleep I have been! As I read…I have been asking myself, 'How did this happen?' and 'When did this happen?'"
>
> —H.T., Hessmer, Louisiana

BVM / Caritas
Medjugorje Pilgrimages

Think about it. If you could combine every single event for the past thirty years that occurred in Washington D.C., New York, Los Angeles, Chicago, Paris, London and every other place in the world, it would be dwarfed by the event of one single day in Medjugorje. Our Lady, Mary, Mother of Christ, comes to the Earth, blesses the whole world with Her presence and speaks to us with words conveyed directly from God. Wouldn't you like to be part of one of the most important events in the history of Creation?

Why pilgrimage with BVM/Caritas?

* The experience of over 449 trips to Medjugorje!

* Combined experience of over 513 years!

* By the testimonies of our pilgrims, it is repeatedly stated that Caritas is the most spiritual!

* Lowest Fares of anybody for a full-hosted pilgrimage!

* Non-smoking trips (many who smoke and travel with us, offer it up as a sacrifice and receive many graces).

* The Community of Caritas lives in Medjugorje which gives us an in-depth, behind-the-scenes understanding of Medjugorje.

* Sites are prayed at, shown and explained (such as the site where Jakov and Vicka were physically and bodily taken to Heaven from Earth by Our Lady).

* The only interest we have is spiritual profit. None of us are paid to guide you. We do it in response to Our Lady's message in which She requested to **"...sacrifice your lives for the salvation of the world..."** (February 25, 1988)

* Our mission house in Medjugorje distributes our materials to all who come from around the world. You will benefit on your pilgrimage by the spiritual material, advice, and guidance that will be available to you.

* You stay in the middle of the village by St. James Church, yet on the trail to Apparition Hill ✧**a best location!**✧ On top of that, pilgrimages are scheduled around special apparitions or being in the village when the monthly message to the world is given.

* BVM/Caritas Pilgrimages has remained loyal and centered exclusively on Medjugorje, and pilgrimages only to this holy village. Focus and prayer life has given us a deep understanding about Our Lady's apparitions.

This year, why not visit the village that is changing the entire world?

Please call BVM/Caritas
Pilgrimages for more details
on your full package:
205-672-2000, ext. 218 24hr.

Check out
www.mej.com
& click pilgrimages on the home page.
Growing everyday as the most extensive Medjugorje website in the world.

Ostali naslovi o Gospinim porukama!

(Tiskano na hrvatskom)

Da biste nabavili još primjeraka knjige, posjetite Misijsku kuću Caritasa u Međugorj
(Upute su na unutarnjoj stranici zadnje korice ove knjižice)

Other Titles About Our Lady's Messages!

If you would like more copies of this booklet for distribution at your church, pray group, or for family or friends, etc…please contact your local bookstore, call Caritas of Birmingham–24 hours a day, or fill out the order form at the end of thi booklet.

Other titles in this series by A Friend of Medjugorje:

Title list cont. on next page

See order form in back of booklet for pricing

3K1019 A Blessing to Help Save the World
3K1020 Fallen Field Angel
3K1021 Don't Tell Me What to Do!
K1022 Spanning 2000 Years of History
3K1023 When You Decide for Change
3K1024 Have You Become Complacent or Fallen Asleep?
3K1025 I Don't Like My Cross
K1026 What Do We Do Now?
3K1027 Thy Will Be Done? And Hand to the Plow
3K1028 Our Lady's 7 Steps to…Set the Captives Free
K1029 Who's Driving?
K1030 "I Don't Have to Go to Medjugorje." Reasons Why One Must Go to Medjugorje
3K1031 The Seven Novenas in Preparation for the Five Days of Prayer for the Reconciling of
Ourselves, Our Families, and Our Nation Back to God
K1033 Calling on Heaven (Caritas' prayers)
K1036 Our Lady's Formula for Victory: "Pray, Pray, Pray"
K1037 A Miracle from the Field for Our Nation
K1038 Crisis-Discipline
K1039 Quietism
K1040 Wedding Booklet
K1041 Why So Many Disasters?
K1042 How the Early Church Learned…
K1043 Be Strong! Do Not Relax!
K1044 Some Remarkable things About Our Lady
K1045 You Have Been Called
K1046 Surrender Your Problems to Me
K1047 Two Americas
K1048 Ready"ing" for the Storm
K1049 Judge with Right Judgement
K1050 Confession of a Big Sin
K1051 Razumijevanje Gospinih poruka (prevedeno na hrvatski)
K1052 Međugorje: Ispunjenje svih Marijinih ukazanja (prevedeno na hrvatski)
K1053 Nova arka (prevedeno na hrvatski)
K1054 Kriza–disciplina (prevedeno na hrvatski)
K1055 Međugorje, Mirjana, otkrivena tajna (prevedeno na hrvatski)
K1056 Čednost (prevedeno na hrvatski)
K1057 Gospin recept za pobjedu: Molite, molite, molite! (prevedeno na hrvatski)
K1058 sotona želi uništiti Međugorje (prevedeno na hrvatski)
K1059 Pogled na 2000 godina kršćanske povijesti (prevedeno na hrvatski)
K1060 Vrijeme odluke (prevedeno na hrvatski)
K1061 5. kolovoza: Što činiš za Njezin rođendan? (prevedeno na hrvatski)
K1062 Ulazak u novo vrijeme (prevedeno na hrvatski)
K1063 S Gospom pred raspelom (prevedeno na hrvatski)
K1064 Pripremanje za oluju (prevedeno na hrvatski)
K1065 Ne volim svoj križ (prevedeno na hrvatski)
K1066 54 Day Rosary Novena

Suggested Donation		
1 Copy	Free (pay only $5.00 S&H)	
10 Copies	$4.00	(40¢ ea.)
25 Copies	$8.75	(35¢ ea.)
50 Copies	$15.00	(30¢ ea.)
100 Copies	$25.00	(25¢ ea.)
1000 Copies	$150.00	(15¢ ea.)

Volume orders can be made up of different booklets.
More booklets are being produced monthly at Caritas of Birmingham,
call 205-672-2000 for new titles.

Name_____ Date_____ e-mail_____

Address_____

City_____ State_____ Zip_____ Phone #_____

Method of Payment: ☐Check/Money Order ☐Cash ☐Visa ☐MasterCard ☐Discover

Card#_____ Exp. Date_____

Caritas ID#_____ (Using your ID# will save at least one week of processing on your order in addition to saving this mission thousands of dollars a year. Please use your ID# which can be found above your address with each mailing received from Caritas, or call 205-672-2000.)

Signature_____

Title	Qty.	Price Ea.	Total
	Subtotal		
	S&H		
	Grand Total		

Suggested Donation

1 Copy	Free	(pay only S&H)
10 Copies	$4.00	(40¢ EA.)
25 Copies	$8.75	(35¢ EA.)
50 Copies	$15.00	(30¢ EA.)
100 Copies	$25.00	(25¢ EA.)
1000 Copies	$150.00	(15¢ EA.)

Shipping & Handling

Order Sub-total	U.S. Mail (Standard)	UPS (Faster)
$0-$10.00	$5.00	$9.00
$10.01-$20.00	$7.50	$11.50
$20.01-$50.00	$10.00	$14.00
$50.01-$100.00	$15.00	$19.00
Over $100.00	15% of total	18% of total

For overnight delivery, call for pricing. ***International (Surface): Double above shipping Cost.
Call for faster International delivery.

Send Order and Donation to:

Caritas of Birmingham
100 Our Lady Queen of Peace Drive
Sterrett, AL 35147 USA

or call **205-672-2000 ext. 315** twenty four hours a day!

80